# Moment to Moment

POEMS OF A MOUNTAIN RECLUSE

# Moment to Moment

POEMS OF A
MOUNTAIN RECLUSE

*by David Budbill*

COPPER CANYON PRESS

Printed in the United States of America.

Grateful acknowledgment is made to George Tsutakawa
for the use of his painting on the cover.

The publication of this book was supported by grants from the Lannan Foun-
dation, the National Endowment for the Arts, and the Washington State Arts
Commission. Additional support was received from Elliott Bay Book Com-
pany, Cynthia Hartwig, and the many members who joined the Friends of
Copper Canyon Press campaign. Copper Canyon Press is in residence with
Centrum at Fort Worden State Park.

LIBRARY OF CONGRESS CATALOGING-IN-PUBLICATION DATA

Budbill, David.
Moment to moment: poems of a
mountain recluse / by David Budbill
p.  cm.
ISBN 1-55659-133-0 (alk. paper)
1. Mountain life – Vermont Poetry.
2. Asia – Civilization Poetry.
3. Zen poetry, American.
1. Title.
PS3552.U346 M66 1999
811'.54 – dc21        99-6385
CIP

3  5  7  9  8  6  4  2

COPPER CANYON PRESS
Post Office Box 271
Port Townsend, Washington 98368
www.ccpress.org

By using the less prestigious native script,
Ryōkan made the banner readable to everyone,
not just the highly educated elite.

STEPHEN ADDISS
*The Art of Zen*

# Acknowledgments

Grateful acknowledgment is made to the magazines and presses where some of these poems first appeared: *Cedar Hill Review, The Greenfield Review, Green Mountains Review, The Henniker Review, A Longhouse Reader, The Maine Times, Potato Eyes, The Sun, Vermont Woodlands,* and *West Branch.*

"On the Road to Buddhahood" (broadside in the White Pine Press Signature Editions, 1997).

Epigraph from Octavio Paz in "North Is Nowhere," quoted from *Nineteen Ways of Looking at Wang Wei,* edited by Eliot Weinberger (Moyer Bell, 1987).

Meng Chiao's "Seeing Off Master T'an," translated by Stephen Owen, from *Sunflower Splendor: Three Thousand Years of Chinese Poetry,* edited by Wu-chi Liu and Irving Yucheng Lo (Anchor Books, 1975).

Quotation from Cho Un-húl in "Which of Them Sees More Clearly?" from *The Moonlit Pond: Korean Classical Poems in Chinese,* edited and translated by Sung-Il Lee (Copper Canyon Press, 1998).

The quotation in "What Keeps Me Here?" from Han Shan is from *Cold Mountain: 100 Poems by the T'ang Poet Han-shan,* translated by Burton Watson (Columbia University Press, 1970).

Quotations from Wang Wei in "The Story of Yu-ling" and "So Says Wang Wei" from *Laughing Lost in the Mountains: Poems of Wang Wei,* translated by Tony Barnstone, Willis Barnstone, and Xu Haixin (University Press of New England, 1991).

The quotation in "Letter to Ni Tsan" is from *Wintry Forests, Old Trees: Some Landscape Themes in Chinese Painting,* by Richard Barnhart, from a catalog for a show at China House Gallery, October 26, 1972–January 28, 1973 (China Institute in America, 1972).

Quotations from T'ao Ch'ien are from *The Selected Poems of T'ao Ch'ien,* translated by David Hinton (Copper Canyon Press, 1993).

Quotations from Issa are from *The Spring of My Life and Selected Haiku,* translated by Sam Hamill (Shambhala, 1997).

Quotation from Po Chü-i in "Calling for Po Chü-i" is from *The Jade Mountain: A Chinese Anthology,* translated by Witter Bynner (Alfred A. Knopf, 1929).

# Contents

*xiv*

# Moment to Moment

POEMS OF A MOUNTAIN RECLUSE

*Part*

# ONE

## How He Writes

A gray and drizzling day
here on Judevine Mountain.

The birds and the wind are still,
and he too so dolorous and quiet

even his breath seems shrill.
His life is a vessel of silence

into which now voices begin
to flow. Slowly the vessel fills

like water filling a well. Now
they are calling more clearly,

calling from far below. Now
higher and closer to him. Now

the vessel is filled. Now it is
brimming over and his pen

floats on the brimming voices.
It follows wherever they go.

## What It Is Like to Read the Ancients

There was a man who left the city, went away into the mountains,
built a cabin and lived in it. He said nothing and saw no one, except
an occasional friend who came to visit, eat a meal of stew, and leave.
After a while when friends arrived they would not see the man,

but they always found a pot of stew cooking on the stove, and
since they were hungry, they ate, then waited for their friend.
When he did not return, they left saying how sorry they were
that they had missed him and vowed to return to see him again.

Year after year the friends returned. Each time they found the stew
but not the man, and always they filled their bowls and ate.
This happened two thousand years ago on a remote mountainside
in China. Yet even today the man's cabin remains, not far from here,

clean, well kept, the woodshed full of wood, a pot of stew
cooking on the stove. I was there just yesterday to fill my bowl.

## Always in These Ancient Chinese Paintings

Always in these ancient Chinese paintings, the rocks, the sky, the fog,
    the endless mountains loom
        over the tiny humans

down there fishing in those boats upon that peaceful river down there
    in the lower right-hand corner, or
        there they barely are

climbing up that narrow mountain path, up and up, fading into
    those remote and towering mountains
        way over on the left,

and always, always you have to look and look before you find
    the little people lost as they are
        in mist and distance,

in that expanse of rock, sky, trees, of mountains and rivers without end,
    and always you can barely see them, which,
        of course, is as it should be.

## On the Road to Buddhahood

Ever plainer. Ever simpler.
Ever more ordinary.

My goal is to become a simpleton.

And from what everybody tells me
I am making real progress.

*Part*

# TWO

## After Thirty Years

Thirty years in one place.
Thirty vegetable gardens in the same soil.
Thirty woodsheds filled and emptied.
Thirty years through the woods and mountains
on the same trails.

This is an age of frantic travel and people think
I am a fool for never going anywhere.
It's okay. I don't care.
In another time I would have been a sage
for doing what I haven't done.

# Another Kind of Travel

While you run all over the world looking for something
  you will never find,
I stay at home and travel all over Judevine Mountain.
  I clamber up the brooks
and into the caves, from the highest to the lowest,
  in the dark and
in the light, I go to places where I've never been and
  all of this within
what seems familiar, old and new, comfortable and
  dangerous, all
right here at home. And every evening when I get back
  to my house and while
I eat my rice and vegetables I look out at the slopes
  of Judevine Mountain
where I've just been and I ponder that day's handful
  of little discoveries –
I call them poems – that have come to me by
  never leaving home.

## Quiet and Seldom Seen

Less than four hours southeast to downtown Boston,
less than three northwest to Montreal, less than seven

south to New York City, yet prowling through the mists
among the cliffs on Judevine Mountain are deer and bear,

moose, and some say the reclusive catamount, the panther.
I prowl here too, among these beasts and all the others,

all of us, by nature, quiet and seldom seen together here
in our wilderness surrounded by that other world.

# North Is Nowhere

The solitude of the mountain is so great
that not even the poet himself is present.
OCTAVIO PAZ

North is nowhere, *nihil*, emptiness, and Judevine Mountain is north.
Come to Judevine Mountain and step into oblivion. Lose yourself

in this remote and lonely wilderness. There is no mirror here, no way
to tell where you might end, the others begin. Here you are no one,

only one – with everyone. Come to Judevine Mountain and find out
who you are. Come to Judevine Mountain and disappear.

## A Stillness, Absolute, Profound

I have known a stillness, absolute, profound,
so deep
this pen across this paper makes a racket.

I have known a quiet so complete,
if I turn my head
my hair against my collar makes the only sound.

I may not know the byways of great cities, or the chatter
at the parties
of important people, but here on Judevine Mountain

I have known a solitude and stillness so profound
that my own breath
is the only evidence there is any life around.

## How

A week now and my vocal cords
have not moved –
not to sing, not to speak.

Nor have I heard another.

I am a large bowl clean and empty
into which each day
the world pours itself.

## Where I Live

Where I live is
    emptiness.

Time to watch
    and listen.

Space between
    events and people.

Room for thoughts
    to wander.

There they go –
    drifting

wherever
    they want to.

I've got no discipline at all!

# Nothing Much

Even though the road to Judevine Mountain
is rough and difficult, and sometimes
it's nearly impassable, and God knows,
it's terribly long – once you actually get here,

Judevine Mountain really isn't that much.
It's higher than some of its neighbors, lower
than lots of others. It's not lofty or difficult.
It never has its head in the clouds. It's not

challenging or inaccessible. Actually it's
kind of unobtrusive and undistinguished.
Just a common, ordinary mountain, really.
There's nothing special about it. It's not

much different from any of its neighbors.
Judevine Mountain likes it that way.

## When I Came to Judevine Mountain

When I came to Judevine Mountain
I thought
all my troubles would cease,
but I brought
books and papers – my ambition –
so now, still,
all I know is grief.

## In the Ancient Tradition

I live within the ancient tradition:
the poet as mountain recluse,
withdrawn and hidden,
a life of genteel poverty,
a quiet life of meditation,

which gives me lots of time
to gnash my teeth and worry over
how I want to be known and read
by everyone and have admirers
everywhere and lots of money!

# The Progress of Ambition

When I was twenty-five I wandered the streets of New York
mumbling to myself: *A quarter of a century, and what have I done!*
Then I quit the world, and withdrew into these mountains
so I could lose my self and see the world
with clear and simple eyes, or so I told myself.

Now I'm almost sixty, and even though I practice every day,
it is still almost impossible to stand at the kitchen window
with my cup of tea and an empty mind and watch the sun
rise over the fir trees to the east. *More than half a century
and what have I done!*

## Like the Clouds

Our lives are like the clouds.

We come from out of nowhere,
take some shape a little while,
then disappear.

No wonder we all want
money, power, prestige,
immortality from poetry.

## The Three Goals

The first goal is to see the thing itself
in and for itself, to see it simply and clearly
for what it is.
> No symbolism, please.

The second goal is to see each individual thing
as unified, as one, with all the other
ten thousand things.
> In this regard, a little wine helps a lot.

The third goal is to grasp the first and the second goals,
to see the universal and the particular,
simultaneously.
> Regarding this one, call me when you get it.

## Bathroom Reading: After a Poem by Han Shan

Do you have any poems from Judevine Mountain
in your house? If you don't, go get some.

Pin one to the bathroom wall beside the toilet.

Read it once in a while when you're sitting there.
Maybe it'll bring some comfort or do some good.

*Part*

# THREE

# After Reading Meng Chiao's
## "Seeing Off Master T'an"

There's never any money! All we do is worry and fight.
I wish I could be like Master T'an and go from place to place
begging for someone to pay my

health-insurance premiums, property taxes and car-repair bills,
but I can't. I have to keep pretending there is nothing wrong.
I know that since ancient times

poets have never gotten fat. What I can't comprehend is how
Master T'an could grow old, hungry, and neglected because of poetry,
yet never dry up, never

become nasty, sarcastic, or bitter. How did he keep his innocence?
How could his sweet and grieving tears, even when he was an old man,
still fall like rain?

# What Would It Be Like?

What would it be like
    not to worry about money?
What would it be like to know
    that there would always be enough?

What would it be like never to see
    that vision of tomorrow
and everything gone and you gone too
    out there on the road and in the wind

with nothing?

## Which of Them Sees More Clearly?

Poet, aristocrat, man of letters, Cho Un-hŭl says:
*Not until noon do I tell my boy to open the brushwood gate.*

Imagine having a servant to open the gate for you.
Imagine being that servant waiting upon your master's whim.

Which of them sees more clearly into the heart of this life?

# No Trail

When I was young I believed my work and passion
would get me where I wanted to go.

Now my hair is falling out, and I know
nothing I have done amounts to anything.

My life is like the bird's path across the sky.
It will leave no trail.

## Variation on a Theme by Another Recluse Who Also Thought about Ambition and the Self

I am nobody.
Who are you?

Do you think
you're nobody too?

## Alone and Lonely

He persists alone and lonely, lost in this wilderness
where he remains in exile, rebellious, defiant, neglected,

or so he imagines. There. You can see him there, every day,
bathing in the private, chilly, satisfying waters of self-pity.

# Three Decades

When I was thirty and just come to the western slopes
of Judevine Mountain to live in solitude and stillness,

to see the world with clear and simple eyes, to cut wood
and garden and make poems, it was exciting to be poor,

and a small price to pay for my independence from the
conniving subterfuge and pathetic intrigue of the academy.

When I was forty and still independent and there was still
no prospect of any financial security, I was yet still glad

to have deer and bear, loons and chickadees for my colleagues,
instead of those who yammer about money all the time. Now

I am on the other side of fifty. My hair is turning white and I am still
poor and full of constant worry. Should I have suffered the academy

a little while for the sake of some security? Oh! what has a life
of whistling duets with white-throated sparrows ever gotten me?

# The Story of Chi Mu Chian

Sometime during the ninth century C.E. in China, the poet
Chi Mu Chian failed his exam and was sent away. He left the city
and went into the mountains knowing he was a failure –
and he was forgotten.

There is only one small reference to him in one
of Wang Wei's poems. His own poems are lost forever
and all because he could not – or would not –
pass the exam.

His poems did not conform to the fashion of the time,
nor did they obey the rules of the academy. His poems
were plain and simple, so blunt and common the literati
didn't even see them.

Only people who didn't matter loved his poems.

## Another Lie

This silence, this emptiness,
this freedom to listen and dream
are all I've ever wanted.

And if that were true my
ambition, bitterness, and envy
would have left me years ago.

## As in Ryōkan's Brushwork

They say Ryōkan's brushwork
was unaffected and free-flowing.

That's the goal of these poems:
no duplicity or guile,

just simple, honest,
direct, and free.

Crisp and clear as a
northern summer dawn.

But, Oh, Brother!
It ain't easy

for a carping, nasty
sophisticate like me!

## You False Masters of Serenity

Damn all you
false masters of serenity,
gurus of the happy.

*Struggle*
is what it means
to be alive and free.

## The Music of My Own Kind Too

Abandoned, stuck, alone and lonely,
exiled from humanity, here on Judevine Mountain.
Only the sounds of raven, coyote, chickadee.

It's not enough! What about the human sound,
the sweetness of the human voice putting words
together into sentences? That's a music too.

I love the songs of raven, coyote, chickadee,
but I'm not them. I need to hear
the music of my own kind too.

## For Wang Wei

At a farmhouse on the Wei River you see cattle wandering home
    along the lane in the afternoon sun.
You see the rugged old man leaning in the doorway of his thatched hut
    watching his son, the herdboy,
as he ambles behind the cattle, a stick in his hand. You see farmers
    returning home, hoes on their shoulders.
They hail each other familiarly. You long for that simple life. You sigh
    and sing the old Confucian song "Oh! to Go Back Again."

From time to time, I sing that song too. But now for me, as then for you,
    there is no going back. The farmhouse is deserted.
The cattle are gone. The old men are dying in nursing homes in the city.
    The sons and daughters are gone. The farmers gone.
No one hails another. Everything has changed.
    Fourteen hundred years of love and grief between us,
yet everything is the same. The old ways are dying still.
    Nothing has changed.

## *Home*


When I was young I dreamed of home and in my dream
I saw a place remote and in the mountains.

Now I'm in that place and I call it home,
yet home is still nowhere I can find.

It must be nowhere is the right place,
and when I get there I'll be home.

## An Unassuming Grandeur

On the other hand, I have a fondness for this place,
an attachment to the climate, the hardship, and the difficulty,

and there is solitude here and quiet,
a kind of modesty in the landscape,

an unassuming grandeur.

## When I Get Depressed

I get silent
　　　and I stare
at nothing
　　　all day long,

or I lie down
　　　and read
the ancient masters
　　　who move me

to even greater
　　　depths of melancholy,
and then,
　　　refreshed, and knowing

I am not alone,
　　　I get up
and join the world
　　　again.

## ON MY FIFTY-EIGHTH BIRTHDAY
## I WRITE TWO POEMS

### *First One:*
### *What Keeps Me Here?*

> Though I look down again on the dusty world,
> What is that land of dreams to me?
> HAN SHAN

Thirty years ago, in a dream, I saw a wild and distant place
where mountain mists are cold and ravens catch the thermals
and then zing on biases across the sky. I found that place.
I cleared a tiny spot out of the wilderness, dug a spring,
built a house, and moved in. And ever since, that is where
I've been – holed up, out of sight, exiled from my own kind.
But I am not Han Shan. I love the world of red dust and the
crush of people therein. Why have I stayed here all these years
among these mountains far from the city? What keeps me here
in this lonely place separated from the world I love?

### *Second One:*
### *I Am Still Here Because for Example*

On a summer morning when I step out and walk
across the dewy grass into the rows of my garden
as my vegetables awake and yawn toward another
summer day and the tree swallows twitter above
my head and the purple finches sing their intense
and liquid songs and the robins cluck across the lawn,

mourning doves low and chickadees scold and above
all that the ravens have come from their lofty aeries
to the east again this morning to see what's changed
since yesterday and, oh, how they croak and chortle
among themselves editorializing on what I have done,
and when, high above the ravens, the red-tailed hawk,
whose nest is in the yellow birch which hangs out over
the waterfall just beyond the garden where the deep
woods begin, when the red-tailed hawk cries and all
those other birds sing and I wander among the rows
of my various green friends stretching themselves into
the summer toward what they were meant to be and
the day dawns peaceful and calm and warm, then –
then I know why, after thirty years, I still live among
these mountains far from the city.

# The Story of Yu-ling

Wang Wei spent his life torn between his need for power and prestige,
wealth and influence in the government, and his desire for
the eremitic life of poverty, withdrawal, and meditation.

The poet Yu-ling, on the other hand, loved country life and shunned
official posts. Once the King of Chu sent for Yu-ling and offered him
a lot of money to serve in the King's government, but Yu-ling,
preferring his life at home working as a gardener and woodcutter,
refused the King's offer of wealth and influence in the capital,
and stayed, instead, at home in poverty and anonymity.

We know of Yu-ling's story only because Wang Wei was
magnanimous enough to write it down. If it weren't for Wang Wei,
Yu-ling's story would be lost forever. Yet we notice also that
only Yu-ling's story survives. No one knows any of his poems.

In one of Wang Wei's poems he says, *Lonely Yu-ling is merely
pailing water for his garden.* Why does Wang Wei say *lonely;*
why does he say *merely?* Is watering a garden
not as important as the actions of a government official?

And would I be asking these questions if it weren't for
the government official who loved poets and the reclusive life
and thus gave us the story of Yu-ling?

## Li Po and Wang Wei

On the one hand,
Li Po in the city –
drunk and loving women all night long
then falling into the river and drowning himself
because he wants to embrace the moon.

On the other,
Wang Wei in the country –
ascetic and vegetarian,
severe and withdrawn, at his hermitage
sitting cross-legged and calm.

And then there's me,
The Fool –
loving and trying to be
them both.

## Be Glad

Why become wise
    when you can be stupid?
Why become sophisticated
    when you can be simple and original?

If you are artless and ordinary,
    the literati, who recognize only
artifice and self-consciousness,
    will ignore you.

Be glad with just a cup of tea,
    a bird's song,
a small book of plain poems,
    and your anonymity.

## How and Why You Should Be Circumspect about Your Inner Life

Try not
to look like you're
on the path to somewhere.

That way
nobody will ask you
where you are going.

# Dilemma

I want to be
      famous
so I can be
      humble
about being
      famous.

What good is my
      humility
when I am
      stuck
in this
      obscurity?

## So Says Wang Wei

When the Emperor is a sage
There are no hermits,
so says Wang Wei –

which is why I've spent
the past thirty years
hiding in these mountains.

## How It Is

The true hermit
answers the phone
on the first ring.

## What's the Difference?

Jade mountains or green,
    Chinese or American,
        eighth century or twentieth,

Cold Mountain
    or Judevine Mountain –
        what's the difference?

Still, the poet
    mad and alone
        in a wilderness of mountains

moaning about his fate
    yet singing still
        the melancholy sweetness

of this life.

## Bugs in a Bowl

Han Shan, that great and crazy, wonder-filled
Chinese poet of a thousand years ago, said:

*We're just like bugs in a bowl. All day*
*going around never leaving their bowl.*

I say, That's right! Every day climbing up
the steep sides, sliding back.

Over and over again. Around and around.
Up and back down.

Sit in the bottom of the bowl, head in your hands,
cry, moan, feel sorry for yourself.

Or. Look around. See your fellow bugs.
Walk around.

Say, Hey, how you doin'?
Say, Nice bowl!

## Such Self-Indulgence and Sloth!

All morning I sit at my desk drinking tea,
reading ancient poets,
and writing my own ridiculous poems.

In the afternoon I go wandering through the woods
to see wildflowers and listen to birds
and the wind singing through the trees.

Then I sit beside the brook down in the bottom
of the ravine where the rock outcroppings loom
over my head, and I listen to the waterfall.

Such self-indulgence and sloth make me so happy!
I wonder who will pay me to be useless and in love.

## Ryōkan Was a Beggar

Ryōkan was a beggar
wandering from place to place

trying to support his poetry
with his begging bowl.

I'm a beggar, in my own way, too,
a hustler and a huckster also.

Poems for sale. Won't you buy
my poems? Poems for sale.

Come, buy my poems.
Take me home with you.

*Part*

# FOUR

## After Li Yi

Everything fades away.
The grass is brown.

My head is bald.
What hair is left is gray.

My youth is gone.
The end of life is in the mirror.

## My Face

My face is falling off.
My face is sliding down my face
and gathering in lumps
on my jaw and under my chin.

My face is sliding down my face
as if my flesh were wet dough
dripping off my skull.
My face is falling off

so that my other face,
the face within, can show
that final, eyeless fellow
with the toothy grin.

## My Old Woman

Even at my advanced age
there are young women,
and not-so-young ones too,

who offer me strange breasts, new arms,
and sweet mysterious thighs.

But my old woman's got a hold on me,
and I am saved from becoming
just another old fool.

As I bless her, thank her, I ask myself:
*What's wrong with just another old fool?*

# After Reading a Poem from The Book of Songs

In her left hand she holds her breast.
With the fingers of her right hand
she gestures for me to come near.

She smiles at me. She says to me,
*Come. Let us lie down together.*
*Let us lie together naked all day.*

She says, *Come to me, my lover.*
*Come, lie here with me. Let us*
*enjoy each other while we can.*

# Letter to Ni Tsan

Ni Tsan, I've been looking at your painting and reading about it too:
*On a rainy windblown day in the fourth lunar month of a year*
*sometime around the middle of the fourteenth century, the*
*painter Ni Tsan, in a state of melancholy depression, was visited*
*by two friends who brought gifts of wine and small delicacies.*

Then the three of you sat together in your pavilion
and drank the wine, ate the delicacies, and visited.
Before your friends went on their way, you made for them,
to show your gratitude, a small painting, ink on paper,
a hanging scroll – the image of an old tree, moss-covered
and vine-grown, gnarled and beaten, wounded and scarred,
and otherwise made beautiful. Beside the old tree stands
a weathered rock. And all around these two ancients,
young and tender sprigs of bamboo reach into the air.
On the painting – Ni Tsan, do you remember? –
you wrote a poem:

> *Wind and rain! Oh! these spring days of gray and chill.*
> *What is left for me after the long winter but to fight*
> *with my depression?*

> *With my brush in my hand as if it were a sword I make*
> *copies of poems, I paint rocks and trees, I make war*
> *against the melancholy I have always known.*

> *Yet there is still something left for me on which I can depend.*
> *Here, these friends who come to cheer me, to bring me gifts:*
> *themselves, wine, and meat with bamboo shoots,*

*all of it meant to quicken my appetite, and it does! It all*
*makes me feel alive. In the midst of all my deepening sorrow,*
*in the midst of all this vernal gloom,*

*I am grateful for this comfort, this brief pleasure with friends.*

Ni Tsan, I am no ancient, not yet, but nonetheless
I too have known sorrow and melancholy, a lifelong sadness,
yet I have also known the comfort of a friend
who comes to me, who reaches out and touches me,
who brings the gift of herself, the wine of her lips,
and other small delicacies. When she visits me, I too feel alive again,
even in the midst of my sorrow, and I am
humbled and grateful for the sweet comfort that she brings.

Ni Tsan, nothing has changed, there is still only sorrow,
and from time to time, still, as it was with you,
some relief from sorrow: this brief pleasure with a friend.

## After Ryōkan's Poem Called "White Hair"

Frost comes at night
    and is gone in the morning.
Snow comes in winter
    and is gone in spring.

But once white hair arrives on your head,
    it never leaves.
Everything else comes and goes
    and comes again.

But not you and me. For us
    it's just this once.
For us, if we're lucky, there is only this
    slow, painful going away.

## The Cycle of the Seasons

The cycle of the seasons is to teach us to prepare
for our own deaths.

We get to practice every year, especially in the fall.
I've had fifty-eight practice sessions now.

But I'm not getting anywhere.
I can't seem to get it.

The more I practice, the older I get,
the less I want to die.

# All of Us

Out of the undifferentiated Tao
come the ten thousand things:

the bug in the bird's mouth,
the bird in the tree,
the tree outside the window,
the window beyond the chair,
the chair in the room,
the man in the chair

who has just risen from the chair
and walked across the room
to look out the window
at the bird in the tree
with the bug in its mouth.

See how all of us,
at our own and different speeds,
return to the Tao.

Oh, let us all
sing praises now for all of us,
so briefly here.

*Part*

# FIVE

## Trying to Be Who I Already Am

People tell me I am arrogant and pigheaded,
    narrow-minded and vain
because I won't follow this week's guru into his
    seventeen steps for improving my life.

Well, I'm over here in a different place –
    with T'ao Ch'ien who says,
*My nature comes of itself. It isn't something*
    *you can force into line.*

So, please, leave me alone.
    I don't want your advice.
I'm just trying to be
    who I already am.

# My Fate Is to Rebel

If you say yes,
I'll say no.

If poetry is this,
I'll write not-this.

## Flawed Verse:
## After a Poem by Han Shan


Vinegar Bob, The Academic, laughs at my flawed verse and says,
*He writes short stories, then chops up the lines so he can pretend*
*they're poems.*
    I say: What's wrong with short stories?

Vinegar Bob, The Academic, laughs at my flawed verse and says,
*He has no command of prosody. He just throws words down*
*anywhere on the page.*
    I say: Yeah, that's right. I'll throw 'em down anywhere I like.

## An Age of Academic Mandarins

This is an age of academic mandarins
who manufacture secret vocabularies
so they can keep their verses to themselves
and away from ordinary people
who could never understand the erudition
of their obtuse allusions, or the quirky twists
of their self-indulgent minds.

Ah, Po Chü-i, how they would laugh at you,
My Friend, standing there in your kitchen
testing your poem on your illiterate cook to see
if it is plain enough so that she and people like her
will be able to comprehend what you have to say.

And when she says she doesn't know what you
are talking about, you go back to your study
to make it plainer, more easily accessible –
pure, clean, simple: so anyone can understand.

# Note to Myself

Never be deliberately obscure.
Life is difficult enough!
Don't add to the confusion.

# Which?

As everybody knows, Keats said:
> *"Beauty is truth, truth beauty" – that is all*
> *Ye know on earth, and all ye need to know.*

Oh yeah?

Lao Tzu said:
> *True words are not beautiful.*
> *Beautiful words are not true.*

Now what?

## Pao Chao and Now

I'm sick of everyone playing the World Series of Poetry,
with poets now or in ancient China, saying undoubtedly
the two greatest poets in Chinese history are Tu Fu and Li Po.
Phooey! There were hundreds of wonderful poets, thousands
of wonderful poems then as now. Why are we always trying
to decide who is the first, the greatest, the best?

For example, have you ever heard of Pao Chao?
He lived and wrote in the wrong time, after T'ao Ch'ien,
before the T'ang. Almost nobody knows him. His poems
are lost in a dark age between the so-called great writers,
yet here his poems are for anybody to read, bitter and loving,
heartfelt and sad, filled with sweetness and regret.

# Teapots as Visions of How Poetry and the World Might Be

My old teapots, some handmade, some mass-produced,
are all *wabi* pots: tea-stained, worn, chipped and cracked,
held together by jagged lines of epoxy: all used and loved.

Now I've got a new teapot: mass-produced, blue-and-white,
the rice pattern, spout that doesn't drip, comfortable handle:
ordinary, functional, elegantly simple, common, and cheap.

*Part*

# SIX

# The Sixth of January

The cat sits on the back of the sofa looking
out the window through the softly falling snow
at the last bit of gray light.

I can't say the sun is going down.
We haven't seen the sun for two months.
Who cares?

I am sitting in the blue chair listening to this stillness.
The only sound: the occasional gurgle of tea
coming out of the pot and into the cup.

How can this be?
Such calm, such peace, such solitude
in this world of woe.

# Snowshoes on Judevine Mountain

Late afternoon and down off Judevine Mountain. My snowshoes:
two ships running side by side and I a colossus straddling the two.
They breast the frothy deep, pushing waves of foam out before
themselves; two snow ships, one and then the other forward
plowing this white and airy sea and I above them through
the darkening woods sweating in the zero cold heading home.

Darker now, sun going down, moon already risen, darker still
and cold dropping down. There. A house in the wilderness.

The house lights glow orange and warm in the evening dark.
Through the door I see rumpled coats hanging in the mudroom.
The house calls, saying, *Come in. Take off your snowshoes,*
*put them in the woodshed, stomp off that snow and come inside.*

*We have a fire in the stove, hot tea in the pot. Take off your*
*snowy clothes. It's warm in here. Supper will be ready soon.*

## Laid Up in Bed

I drink tea, read Issa, Confucius, Yuan Mei.
The white pine outside my window
bows gracefully under its load of snow.

Quiet room, warm covers, warm cup.
Fragrance of oolong,
the sound of a page turning.

## What Happened Today:
## The Twentieth of January

Far out into the woods the dog and I out for a hike up an
eastern slope of Judevine Mountain, an hour up, an hour back,

then the dog finds a moose antler only a little eaten, a treasure,
our prize, only the second antler in thirty years of roaming –

usually the rodents get them first – pure calcium, you know – then
home through the dying light hauling half a forty-pound moose-rack,

the ravens and I set up a yammer – they circle around and around
wondering what this croaking, half-assed imitation of themselves

is doing. We talk and talk, back and forth – almost
all the way home. Obviously we've got something going here.

I just wish I knew what we were saying.

## Haiku and Tanka for Shrike

Two hundred years ago and
half the world away Issa said:
*His patience expired,*
*from high in his treetop*
*the old shrike cries.*

Again. Here. Today.

All morning the shrike
waited in the apple tree
for a chickadee
to forget. Then he, fed up,
so to speak, went on his way.

## The First Green of Spring

Out walking in the swamp picking cowslip, marsh marigold,
this sweet first green of spring. Now sautéed in a pan melting
to a deeper green than ever they were alive, this green, this life,

harbinger of things to come. Now we sit at the table munching
on this message from the dawn which says we and the world
are alive again today, and this is the world's birthday. And

even though we know we are growing old, we are dying, we
will never be young again, we also know we're still right here
now, today, and, my oh my! don't these greens taste good.

## After a Walk on a Gray, Drizzling, Cold Spring Morning: The Thirtieth of April

There: below me in the wet, brushy place
year after year, generation after generation,
the woodcock whistle and snout.

And there: on only slightly higher ground
the veeries warble and sing their liquid
descending glissando, year after year.

And here: almost beside me, the shy junco
scurries, flits across the ground singing
again this spring only: tick, tick, tick, tick.

And I too in this orchestra. I too. No more,
no less than they, making again my own song
with these marks, this paper, these words.

Each in our own place, each in our own time,
each calling distinctly, all calling together.
Sublime and earthy. This chorus of voices.

In concert together making this song.

## What I Did Today:
## The Sixth of May

I stacked rough-cut lumber. I worked on a new poem.
I wrote a letter to a friend. I talked on the phone.

I watched the birds feeding at the feeder.
I ate rice and dal. I thought about how old I'm getting.

I read some poems.
I thought about my father's death.

I thought about my own death. I took a nap.
I read some poems.

I walked two miles in the rain.
I filled the bird feeders.

I drank tea.
I watched darkness fall.

## During the Warblers' Spring Migration, While Feeling Sorry for Myself for Being Stuck Here, the Dooryard Birds Save Me from My Melancholy

I am not a rare warbler,
brilliant migratory avatar,
here only momentarily
to sing
a brilliant song.

I am a common chickadee
a long time here to sing
a common song about
how beautiful
the ordinary is.

## The End of Winter

The delicate and lovely emptiness of winter
gone now today, suddenly gone,
this last week
of May.

The glut of summer rushes in,
grass crowding everything,
trees thick again
with green.

The whole world full of life and noise
closing in, and nowhere for us
dark ones, depressed ones,
to hide.

# After Reading Ou-yang Hsiu's Poem Called "Spring Walk to the Pavilion of Good Crops and Peace"

It is beginning again. The Pavilion of Good Crops and Peace
has decorated itself again. The hills are green. The garden
is full of young shoots. The sun is high and warm. Already
countless generations of wildflowers have gone to seed.

I can hear music coming from the pavilion. It floats on the air
like apple blossoms falling, like spring birds singing in midair.
The peas and beans, the young maple leaves are singing.
*Warmth and peace. Life to all that grows.*

But there is no peace.

In 1961 I stepped onto Hough Avenue in Cleveland, Ohio, and saw
a man lying on his back on the sidewalk bleeding. I saw another man
standing over him. Then the standing man raised his foot and
stomped it down on the other man's face. When he took his foot away
the other man's face was gone. The standing man wiped his shoe
on the other man's shirt and walked away.

Yet the music still comes. It floats on the air.
The peas and beans, the young maple leaves will not quit singing.
They will not give up their song.
*Warmth and peace. Life to all that grows.*

## *What Good Does It Do?*

What good does it do to live and write
    from Judevine Mountain
when no one anymore knows or even
    cares about the seasons?

When my ancient-Chinese brothers
    made their poems people knew
what spring meant; they knew
    the verdant and salubrious grace

of summer, the autumnal melancholy
    of the cricket and the
chrysanthemum. But now, every day
    for everyone is just the same,

a time to get and spend. No one cares about
    or even notices the clouds,
the angle of the sun, or in the summer
    how green things strive

and so often fail to become
    what they were meant to be.

# All Summer

All summer, while poets go from one writers' conference to another
teaching the ways of poetry, Judevine Mountain stays home.

He tends his broccoli and tomatoes, rears his potatoes and beans,
cultivates his corn and cuts a year's supply of firewood.

He has a summer conference of his own with his vegetables,
and he is well-known to the hummingbirds, resident robins,

cedar waxwings, and a family of tree swallows who live above
the garden in a box that he provided for the bluebirds. Each

morning he whistles a duet with the white-throated sparrow who
lives in the balsam fir just below the road, and late in the afternoon

an indigo bunting comes to eat the seeds of the tall grass that grows
beside his house, and never does he utter a word to anyone about poetry.

## Ahimsa Next Time Maybe
### *or*
### The Taoist Mountain Recluse
### Stands in His Summer Garden and
### Says to the Deerfly About to Bite Him

*Back to the undifferentiated Tao,*
*you son of a bitch!*

And he smashes the triangular fly
into the hairs on his dirty brown arm.

# The Young Woodchuck

His burrow emerged from underground exactly between
two hilled rows of potatoes, and for ten days after he
first broke through to daylight, he must have thought he'd
arrived in Shangri-La, in Beulah Land – the opening to his burrow
protected by the dense foliage of potatoes, and two feet away
pumpkin and squash, a row of parsley, succulent leaves
of green beans, Swiss chard, collard greens, four kinds of lettuce,
and rows of cabbages and broccolis, and for dessert the pungent leaves
and flowers of marigold: high summer, warm and bright and this
cornucopia of food – until yesterday.

At midday I waited for him to appear, and when he did, when he
sat up and looked around, as they always do, I put the shotgun
to my shoulder and sent a charge of pellets through his ear.

Death come from out of nowhere. Ten days in paradise and suddenly
only his body in that agony; he on his back, his legs pawing the air
as if he were already digging a burrow in another place.

# To a Friend

Michael, you know we will never do enough to save ourselves.
And it is all too clear that the world goes on without us.
Therefore, My Friend, let us give up this madness and vanity
and go up to where the Moose River snakes through Victory Bog,

to where we can sing with Li Po and say:
> Since water still flows, though we cut it with swords,
> And sorrow returns, though we drown it with wine,
> Since the world can in no way satisfy our cravings,
> Let us loosen our hair tomorrow and go fishing.

# Old Red Beard, My Friend

Old Red Beard, My Friend, who lives in exile and whom I never see,
how I wish you could come to my house this summer
and sit on the porch with me.

We could drink tea, eat candied ginger, and, late in the afternoon,
watch the swallows swooping low over the vegetable garden
catching insects

as dusk comes on. Then after the swallows have gone to bed
and we have had our supper, the dragonflies will come out
and do their swooping also,

only higher up in the air so that we will lift our cups toward
the heavens and toast them again and again, cheer them on –
Go to it! Bug Patrol! –

while we sit getting drunker and drunker on the beauty of this world
as the evening settles down around us and the mountains to the east
turn purple. And when

it is dark and we have lighted the lamps on the porch, we will
remember, in the stillness of the night, our ancient-Chinese brothers
who, thousands of years ago,

also fell in love with beauty and grew old and made also such
melancholy poems about the fleeting sweetness of this life.

## Old Poet Refuses to Leave Home

My Friend, Red Beard, is getting famous now; now, that is, that he is over seventy. He got invited to Bellagio, to Italy, a villa, servants, the Rockefellers, rich food, stuffy people, this place where you must dress for dinner every night and promenade around with a glass of sherry and talk to important personages – prestige and contacts, power, influence, who knows what else!

Red Beard actually planned to go: it would be nice, a vacation, people to wait on you, hand and foot, day and night, your every need, a break from the daily drudgery, the routine. Then he realized he'd have to spend his days with all those, as he put it, "shirty internationals," which is to say sometimes even a master can be distracted momentarily by the distractions of this world, but, because he is a master, he regained his equilibrium, knowing that daily drudgery is the mantra of his life, the source and wellspring of his poems.

And so it was that Red Beard left his so-called friends baffled, open-mouthed and consternated, and stayed home, stayed in his little dump on his little hillside in upstate New York where he could sweep up wallboard dust from the recent remodeling, and shovel snow and plan the summer garden and sit at the table in the kitchen all day long and smoke and watch the birds out the window at the feeder as they come and go and listen to the voices from within and be alone and once in a while write down a line or two that maybe sometime, maybe someday, might be a part of some new poem.

## One Summer Afternoon Many Years Ago While Visiting My Friend Joel, Who Is Dead Now, at His House Which We Called The Depressive Poet's Rehabilitation Center, I Wrote this Poem

Joel and I together – just two old friends with nothing much to do –
sit at the table and talk, eat lunch and talk – about poetry and women,
ambition and jealousy. And then take a little nap.

Awake now and sleepy, my hands behind my head, a breeze
through the open window. The sky darkens beyond the skylight.
Then… it's nice how the rain sounds on the roof. Listen.

Cars go by, their tires make that noise on the wet road.
And then, some children, far off, laughing, after the rain.

## After Labor Day

Summer people gone.
Kids back in school.

Fall coming fast.
Leaves turning.

Birds going south.
World getting quiet.

Chinese melancholy.
Sweet Zen emptiness.

Here again this year.

# Harmonizing with Tu Fu's
## "Written on the Wall at Chang's Hermitage"

It is fall here now in the mountains. The air is crisp and bright.
Time for cutting wood. First the chainsaw's whine, then the
splitting hammer's fall, the clunk of blocks of wood coming apart.

I pause from my labors, wipe the sweat from my face,
and look down the hill to my late garden and then across
the valley to the yellow side of Judevine Mountain.

I am alone here today and I want to be alone. To cut, split,
and stack firewood, to eat simple food I myself have grown,
to work with pen and paper or at my computer making poems,

to sit in the evening and listen to the silence of these mountains:
these simple things, the warmth of friends, and love – the touch
of another – are all I've ever wanted. All else is distraction.

## Autumn and Crickets

The autumn air, chill and clear,
moves in to stay.

The crickets, so sad and beautiful,
sound all day.

## For Owl Wing

Fall has come, My Friend. The air is cold, the sky
is crystalline, the hills transformed from green to

yellow and red, and I transformed from gardener
to woodcutter. Today as I stand here on this hillside

working on my woodpile I pause and see for thirty miles
off through the clear air. Owl Wing, My Friend, how I

wish you could come to visit me. We could take a day
and hike into the hills. I know a place where a stream

begins high up toward the top of Judevine Mountain
where we could build a little fire, boil some tea, eat

some cakes we'd made that morning. Then we could sit
leaning up against a tree, our faces toward the dying light,

and talk of poetry and women, regret and loneliness,
of disappointment and of love.

## After Reading Po Chü-i's
## "Drunk, Facing Crimson Leaves"

Now the year dies again. The hills are red and yellow again.
The geese go over crying, *Good-bye! Good-bye!* again.

See how sweetly the year dies, how willingly it accepts its fate.
With such loveliness and grace it succumbs to the inevitable.

And why shouldn't it? It knows in just a few short months
it will be alive again, young and green and wet and spring again.

There is no such hope for me. My fate is to grow old and die
and never see these colored hills again, never hear the geese again.

Why? Why all this only once for me? Why can't my life
be a circle also and not this line I travel toward oblivion?

## Stillness, O Stillness

Low clouds and gray, cold and spitting snow,
more like the first of November than October first
except for the geese going over low all morning.

Their frantic cries of leaving fill me with a quiet joy.
The world gets emptier, more barren, and I more alone.
Stillness, O stillness, this damp calm of autumn, this

relinquishing, giving in, gray turning toward winter,
sweet melancholy, welcoming, opening, acceptance,
receiving, this embrace of the quiet and the dark.

## Melancholy Thoughts

Today while walking through the rainy woods heading home
all I can think about is how all too soon I will be gone
and never will I walk again beneath

these barren, rain-soaked trees, never will I pad again
over these soft and quiet leaves, never return
home again to stand beside the warming stove,

never again be drunk on sadness or on wine.
If only I would never reach the end!
If I could always only be on the Way.

## All the Raucous Birds of Summer

All the raucous birds of summer:
faithless, transitory, fly-by-nights –
finally gone. Sky quiet, ear empty.

Chickadee, companion through
the cold and dark, little friend
at the dooryard feeder again.

Now those of us who stay,
we quiet ones,
settle into the winter.

# Calling for Po Chü-i

All day I have wandered alone
    in these barren, autumnal mountains,
everything, including me,
    dank with mists and full of darkness.

Now back home again;
    only a few coals remain in the stove.
I will build a new fire, drink some tea,
    cook a supper of rice and vegetables.

And I will also remember your poem, Po Chü-i,
    which says: *There's a stir of red in the quiet stove,*
*There's a feeling of snow in the dusk outside –*
    *What about a cup of wine inside?*

O ancient brother and friend, come,
    be here with me this evening.
Keep me company. Come for supper and for wine.
    And after we have had our fill

we'll sit beside the warming stove,
    drinking tea and listening
to the silence of the night together
    here at the beginning of winter.

# In Ryōkan's Company

Here in the shadow of Judevine Mountain where I wander and sit
and sing my own songs, it is bitterly cold tonight. I am home beside
the woodstove with a book of Ryōkan's poems, a pot of tea.

Then it is two hundred years ago and I am sitting and drinking
with my Japanese friend beside another woodstove in another
small house in the shadow of strange mountains far from home.

I close the book and listen to him
sing his poems
into the stillness of the night.

## Small Song of Praise at Christmastime
## for Chickadee

Now we sing
our praises to
tiny chickadee –

chicka-dee dee!
dee dee dee
chicka-dee dee dee!

Close, diminutive,
quiet: in the
bare apple tree.

# A Winter Night

The winter night is dark and cold. The weatherman says
we're in for trouble. What do I care?

The woodbox is full, the cast-iron stove is glowing.
I've got a cup of tea. A pot of water simmers on the stove.

Beside my chair: Pao Chao, Ryōkan, Po Chü-i,
Wang Wei, *The Book of Songs*, some pencils and paper.

Let the wind howl, let the snow come.
I won't think about money or ambition until tomorrow.

Tonight I'll sit here, as Ryōkan did two hundred years
before me, *quietly reading poems from long ago.*

*Part*

# SEVEN

# Who I Love

I love Siddhārtha Gautama, Jesus of Nazareth, and Confucius too, but
mostly who I love is, I mostly love Lao Tzu, because out of him rises

two thousand years of sweet melancholy and desire for this life, this
place, our flesh, the now – the suckling babe, a steaming bowl of rice,

stir-fried vegetables, the lone goose as she flies across the river of the
stars, mists on mountains, a poached fish, the cedar waxwing in the

piney boughs, a lone fisherman in a boat on a pond, the jade shaft
within the jade chamber, lost to the joy of a thousand loving thrusts,

the shouts and sighs, the sweet, ecstatic moans of love, and also, yes,
the graybeard leaning on his cane as he waits to die and the last, sad

bloom of autumn, the chrysanthemum. Oh, I love Siddhārtha Gautama,
Jesus of Nazareth, and Confucius too, but mostly, mostly who I love is

the ancient, earthbound, sensuous Lao Tzu.

# Quoting T'ao Ch'ien

A thousand years may be beyond me
but I can turn this morning into forever.

For thirty years I've studied ancient-Chinese poets
and Taoist texts, and often I have longed to abjure
this world, these days, to see through the red dust
of our fleeting lives and thus accede to immortality.

But, alas and luckily, for me – *character is fate.*
I love this world too much to want to find a way
away from it. I give my soul to my senses.

I love the sound of birds, the sight of wind
passing through the trees, the swollen cock,
the soaking vulva, a bowl of vegetables and noodles,
a cup of wine, the sweet aroma of some tea.

*How could heaven be anywhere but here?*
This place, now, today… is eternity,
and it is here in me and in my dying life.

## On Hearing That These Poems
## Would Be Published in a Book

For every victor, a vanquished,
which is why Lao Tzu says:
*Treat your victory as a funeral.*

Therefore, I bow

in gratitude and sadness
before the unknown someone
whose place I took.

# What Issa Heard

Two hundred years ago Issa heard the morning birds
singing sutras to this suffering world.

I heard them too, this morning, which must mean,

since we will always have a suffering world,
we must also always have a song.

# About the Author

David Budbill was born in Cleveland, Ohio, in 1940 to a streetcar driver and a minister's daughter. He is the author of six books of poems, eight plays, a novel, a collection of short stories, a picture book for children, and dozens of essays, introductions, speeches, and book reviews. *Zen Mountains / Zen Streets*, an audio CD of his poetry, with the music of jazz bassist and composer William Parker, was recently released on the Boxholder Records label. He has also served as an occasional commentator on National Public Radio's *All Things Considered*.

Simultaneous to the publication of *Moment to Moment*, Chelsea Green Publishing Company will be reissuing *Judevine: The Complete Poems*, first published in 1991. The stage version of *Judevine*, based on the book, has now been performed in twenty-two states. The 1990 American Conservatory Theatre production of *Judevine* in San Francisco won the Bay Area Critics' Circle Award for Best Ensemble Performance for that year.

Among David Budbill's other prizes and honors are a National Endowment for the Arts Fellowship in playwriting, a Guggenheim Fellowship in poetry, and a Dorothy Canfield Fisher Award for fiction.

He lives in the mountains of northern Vermont with his wife, the painter Lois Eby.

The Chinese character for poetry (*shih*) combines "word" and "temple." It also serves as raison d'être for Copper Canyon Press.

Founded in 1972, Copper Canyon publishes extraordinary work – from Nobel laureates to emerging poets – and strives to maintain the highest standards of design, manufacture, marketing, and distribution. Our commitment is nurtured and sustained by the community of readers, writers, booksellers, librarians, teachers, students – everyone who shares the conviction that poetry clarifies and deepens social and spiritual awareness.

Great books depend on great presses. Publication of great poetry is especially dependent on the informed appreciation and generous patronage of readers. By becoming a Friend of Copper Canyon Press you can secure the future – and the legacy – of one of the finest independent publishers in America.

*For information and catalogs:*

COPPER CANYON PRESS

Post Office Box 271
Port Townsend, Washington 98368
360/385-4925
coppercanyon@olympus.net
www.ccpress.org

COLOPHON

This book is set in Adobe Jenson, a typeface created for
digital composition by Robert Slimbach in 1995. Jenson
reflects the scribal spirit of typefaces designed in fifteenth-
century Venice by Nicolas Jenson. Book design by Valerie
Brewster, Scribe Typography. Printed on archival-quality
Glatfelter Author's Text at McNaughton & Gunn, Inc.